paperblanks™

A

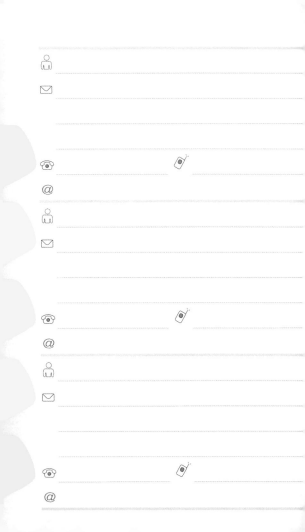

A

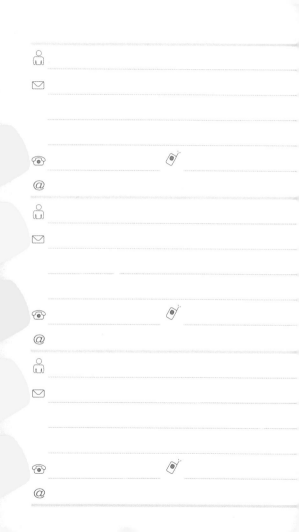

B

B

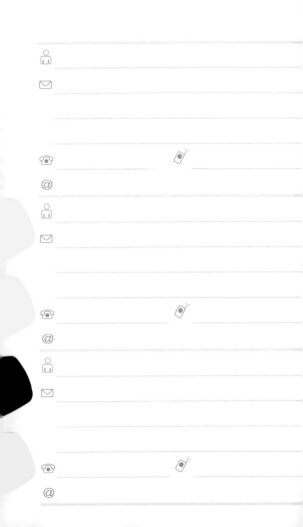

B

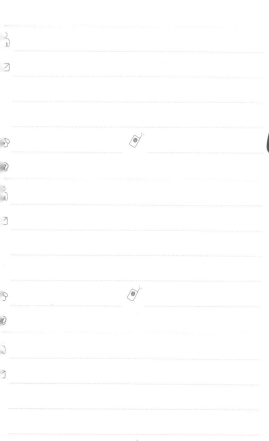

B

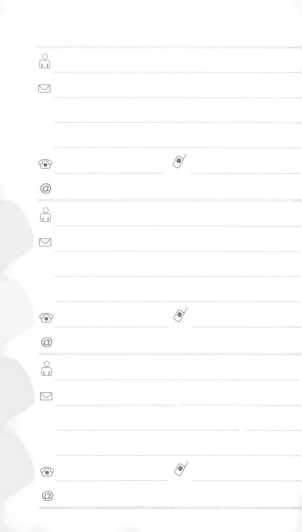

C

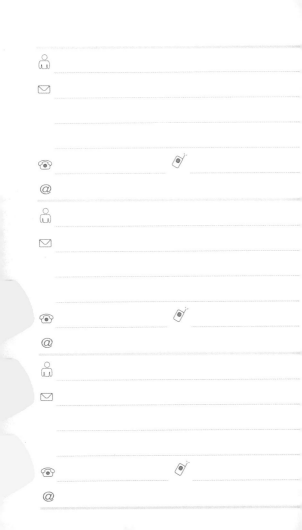

C

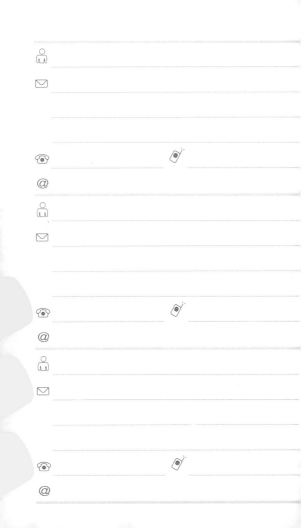

C

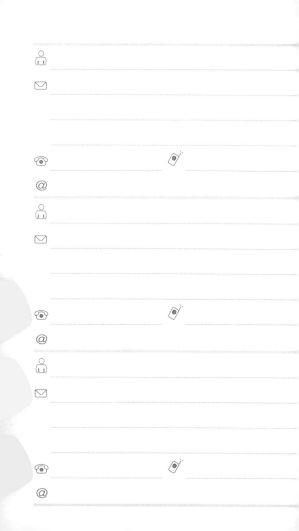

D

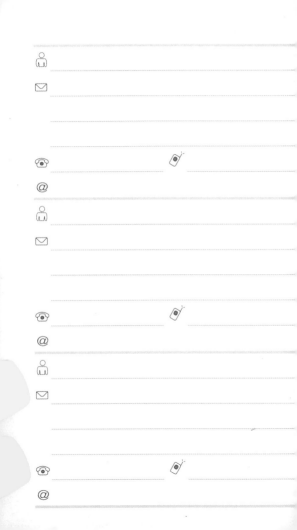

D

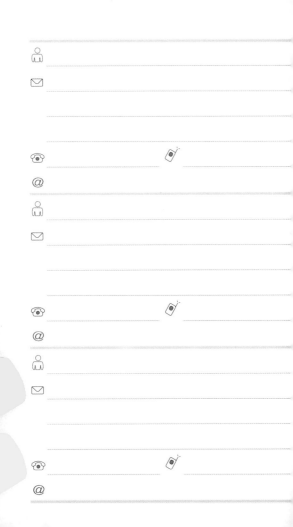

E
F

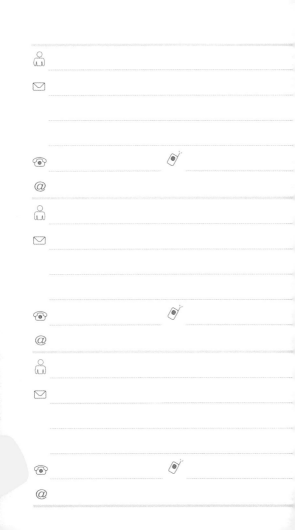

E
F

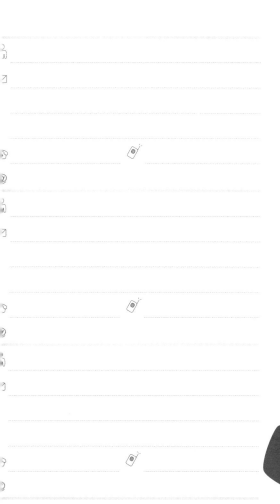

G

H
I

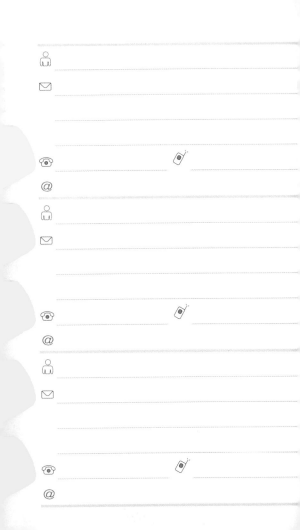

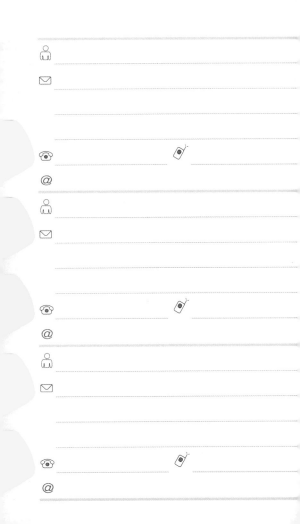

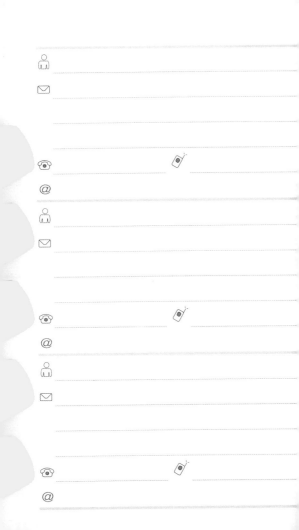

J
K

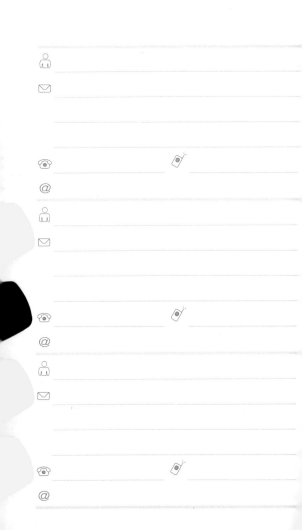

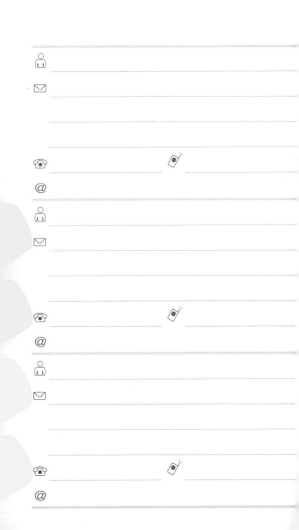

L

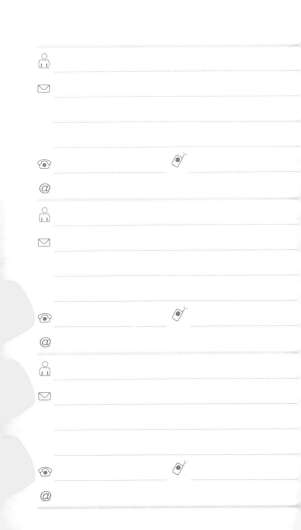

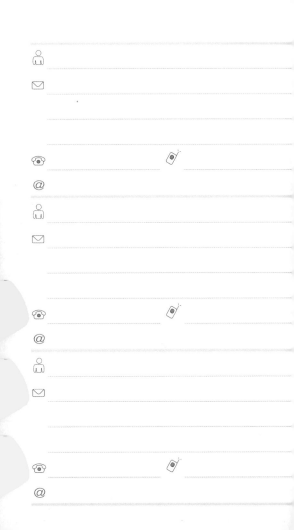

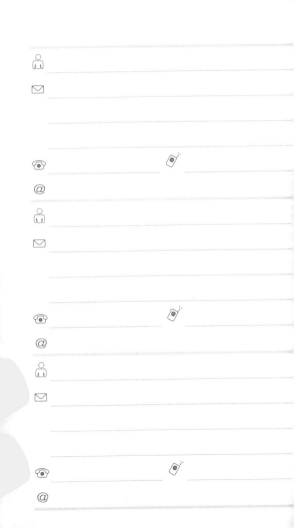

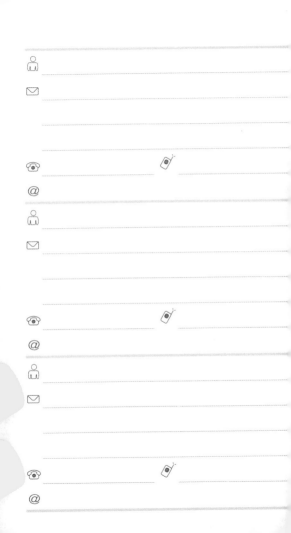

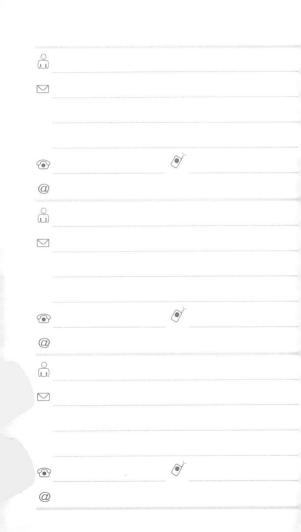

M

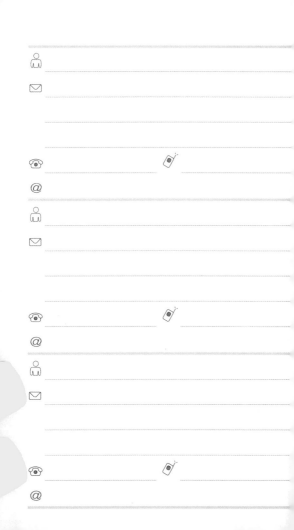

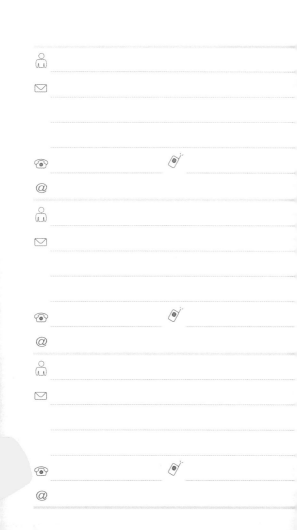

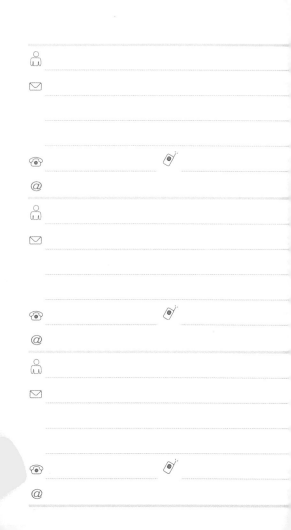

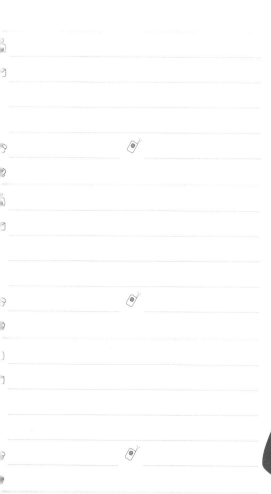

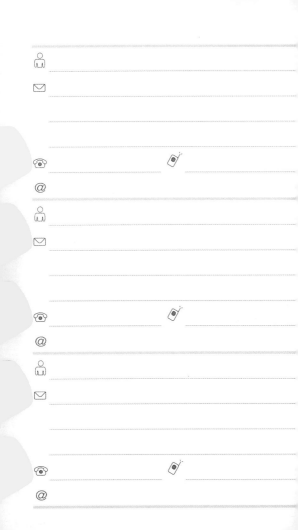

Q
R

Q
R

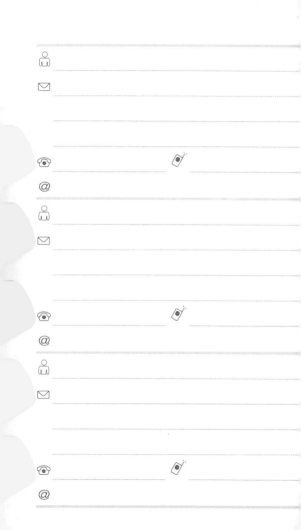

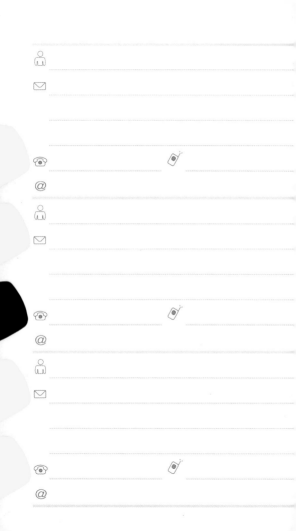

S

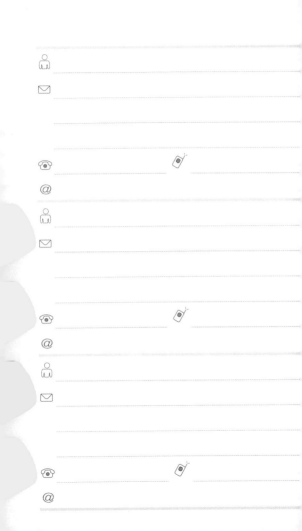

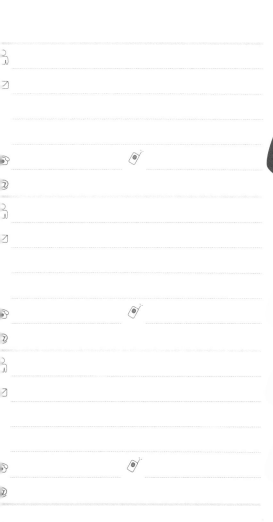

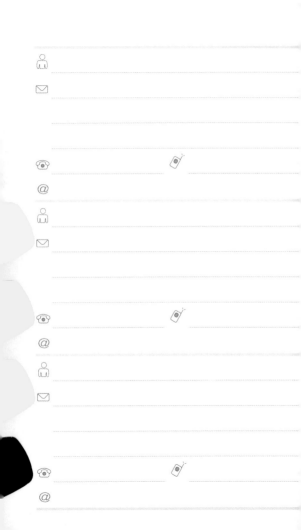

S

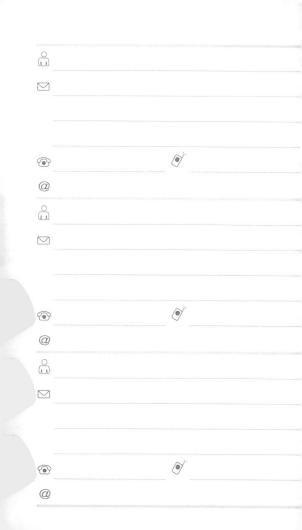

T

U
V
W

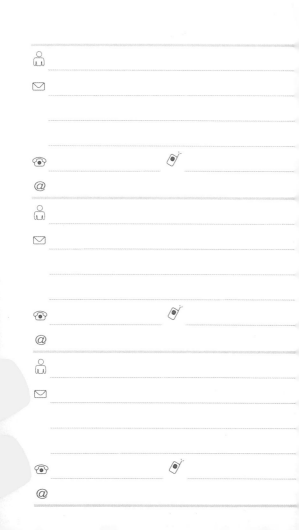

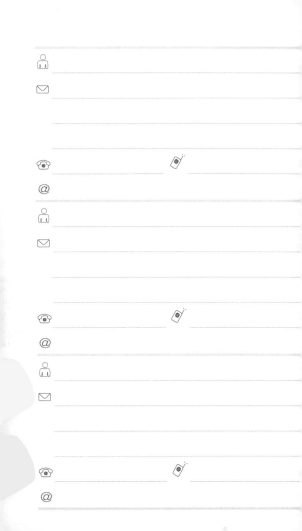

U
V
W

X
Y
Z

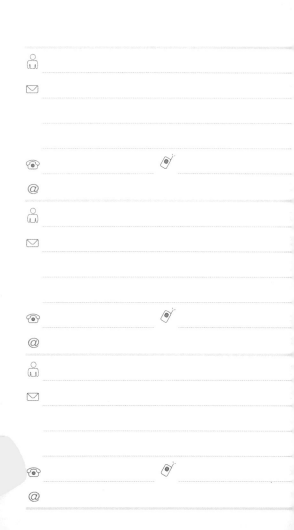

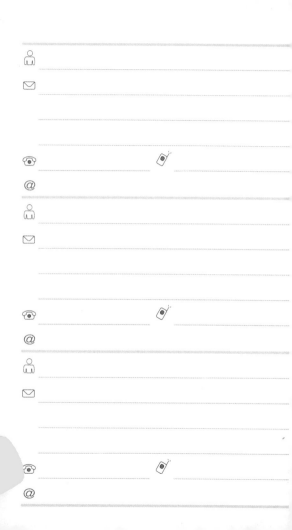

X
Y
Z

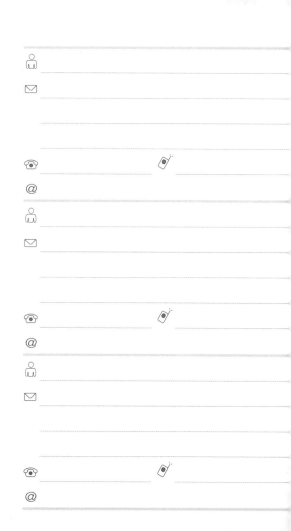

Die Kompositionen von Wolfgang Amadeus Mozart begeistern die Menschen auch mehr als zweihundert Jahre nach seinem Tod. Die Ballettmusik auf der Vorderseite unseres adressbücher aus *La Chasse* (KV 300 [299d]) soll 1778 in Paris komponiert worden sein. Jagdthemen mit erotischem Hintergrund waren damals in Ballett- und Pantomimeaufführungen sehr beliebt. Meist traten darin Schäfer und Schäferinnen auf, die sich mit Amor vergnügten..

La musica di Mozart continua tutt'oggi ad incantare. Si ritiene che la partitura del balletto 'La Chasse', riprodotta sulla copertina del nostra rubrica, sia stata scritta a Parigi nel 1778. I temi dell'inseguimento e della caccia, con un sottinteso significato erotico, e le figure saltellanti di pastori, pastorelle e di Cupido erano popolari nei balletti e nelle pantomime del tempo.

Eteint depuis plus de deux cent ans, Wolfgang Amadeus Mozart continue d'inspirer les mélomanes. Son ballet « La Chasse » (KV 300 [299d]), en couverture de notre répertoire, semble avoir été composé à Paris en 1778. A l'époque, le thème de la chasse souligné d'une touche d'érotisme où bergers, bergères et Cupidon batifolent ensemble, était très en vogue dans les spectacles de ballet et de pantomime.

A más de doscientos años de su muerte, Wolfgang Amadeus Mozart continúa inspirando a los amantes de la música. La sonata La Chasse (KV 300 [299d]), en la cubierta de nuestra libreta de direcciones, se compuso en Paris en 1778; temas de caza con un subtexto erótico, representando a pastores y Cupido jugueteando, fueron populares en representaciones escénicas de la época.

De composities van Wolfgang Amadeus Mozart blijven muziekliefhebbers meer dan tweehonderd jaar na zijn dood inspireren. De balletmuziek getiteld La Chasse (KV 300 [299d]) op deze kaft is waarschijnlijk gecomponeerd in Parijs in 1778. Jachtthema's met een erotische ondertoon waren populair in ballet en pantomime-uitvoeringen in die tijd, met de onvermijdelijke dartelende herders, herderinnen en Cupido.

paperblanks™
ADDRESS BOOKS

Mozart

The compositions of Wolfgang Amadeus Mozart continue
to inspire music lovers more than two hundred years after
his death. The ballet score entitled *La Chasse* (KV 300
[299d]) on our journal cover is believed to have been com-
posed in Paris in 1778. Chasing and hunting themes with an
erotic subtext, typically featuring shepherds, shepherdesses
and Cupid frolicking together, were popular in ballet and
pantomime performances of the time.

ISBN 10: 1-55156-757-1   ISBN 13: 978-1-55156-757-0
MINI FORMAT 128 PAGES

North America 1-800-277-5887
Europe +800-3333-8005

www.paperblanks.com